Franco Dragone

Photography and Text
Jean-Marie Périer

Foreword
Jean-Claude Carrière

Production
Sylvie Flaure/At Large

Photographic Art Direction and Coordination
Sophie Aubry

Book Design
Henri Latzarus

Flammarion

At the threshold of the dream

EVERY DREAM IS A SHOW. A private, intimate show, never to be repeated. At any particular point on any particular night, we may be the privileged subject of a vision. Always a surprise, it comes while we are sleeping and unprepared. This dream of ours does not last for long. It ends as suddenly as it came, without reason, leaving us bitter, frustrated, and awake.

Franco Dragone's dream—*Le Rêve*—is different. It is a carefully, painstakingly prepared work; a coherent and persistent vision in the form of a journey into the unimaginable. It is made to last and is aimed at a vast audience, none of whom should be left with a feeling of disappointment, frustration, déjà vu, or the impression that this dream will be easily forgotten.

This dream is almost the opposite of the dreams we dream at night. This is a dream to have with our eyes wide open.

Franco Dragone is a master at this. He shifts with apparent ease between the real and the elusive, constantly moving from element to element. From humble origins as the son of immigrant Italian workers in a mining town in Belgium, he met with early success as the creator of the Cirque du Soleil and has become, in the eyes of Las Vegas, a prince. And Las Vegas knows a prince when it sees one. Dragone's productions have seen huge box-office success for years. They are sumptuous.

It is worth pointing out that more money is now made in Las Vegas from show business than from gambling. The old image of the town as a den of iniquity lost in the Nevada Desert is slipping away. Everything changes. Schools of mime, drama schools, film schools, and dance academies are all starting up. Could Las Vegas be on the brink of becoming one of the great cultural centers of tomorrow? Not impossible.

Despite his success, Franco Dragone himself has not changed. He remains attached to the Belgian town of La Louvière where he still lives and works. He is always on the alert, curious about everything. He openly states at the beginning of a project that he has, as yet, nothing in mind, that he will wait and see, that he is counting to a great degree on the others involved and aiming for a truly communal performance piece. This miner's son is perfectly at ease working with Steve Wynn, the American billionaire. Wynn is an art lover on a grand scale: the only privately-owned Vermeer in the world is in his collection. In the luxury hotel complex that bears his name—where you can buy anything from a pizza to a Ferrari, and where the rooms are booked up for the next two years—he built a two-thousand-seat theater, custom-made for one show, one dream: the unique *Le Rêve*.

If all goes well, this dream will last for ten years. And when the time comes to wake up, it will be extinguished.

Photographer Jean-Marie Périer shares with us a view from behind the scenes of *Le Rêve,* the unseen and unconscious part of the show. We are witnesses to the merciless selection process, the strangeness of these pyramids of muscle, the grueling preparation, the whole arduous, frustrating quest, as it is renewed every day.

On top of the challenge faced by *Le Rêve*'s dreamer, its creator Dragone, is that faced by the photographer. It is the classic problem of how, in a still image, to communicate the restless quiver of movement. How to freeze a whirlwind. How to persuade silence to hear noise. How can the pages of a book, as we turn them serenely with our fingers, plunge us into the teeth of danger?

Jean-Marie Périer is no stranger to these questions. He has been facing them for a long time. One might even say that they stimulate him, that they are what he lives for.

What the photographer shows here is that the effort has a secret to tell. Not within the effort itself—the meticulous training, the extreme muscle exertion, and the calculated precision of the movements—the secret lies elsewhere. It is to be found, I believe, in the beauty. The desire to create, above all, a "beautiful" photograph, one capable not only of surprising, or even stupefying us, but one which adds something to our sense of wonder in the world. The real world or the world of dreams, little matter which.

The athletes, gymnasts, Olympic champions, and top swimmers undergo a transformation. They change their identity and even their nature. Shaped by a creator and his assistants, they earn the right to be called artists. A new standing, and the prospect of beauty itself as their next trophy.

This metamorphosis, this secret process, has been captured by the photographer, as only he can. Thanks to him, we are able to browse through the book, stopping at a picture for as long as we desire. We can flick through quickly or take time to ponder; turn back the pages, or pick one at random; leave the book open on a table, waiting for a breeze to flip to one page or another in our absence.

Catching us off guard, the immediacy of these figures can be a startling surprise; disturbing because they are unexpected, like the first thing we see in the dreams of night or in the streaming light of day. But this is only a fleeting sensation; the unexpected image soon disappears, only to be replaced by other forms, ever more elaborate, more skillful. Fortunately, the photographer was there to catch them all.

To be receptive to these feelings—which have nothing complicated or inaccessible about them—is to draw something greater than simple pleasure from this book. There can be something reassuring, even comforting about it. We should let ourselves go, get past our sense of surprise. This strange race of beings, embodying impossible balancing acts before our eyes—flinging themselves into nothingness, walking in a void, breathing in water, swimming in air—is, after all, our own race. And, at last, we have a reason to be proud of it.

Before long, the effort seems to have vanished. As if it had been swallowed up, or dispelled, by the beauty. A beauty that gradually becomes more and more apparent. Jean-Marie Périer's photographs effortlessly capture episodes of a work that are displays of pure grace. Everything is easy, everything is harmonious and shared. Everything—pardon the aquatic pun—goes swimmingly.

For us too, the spectators, no effort is necessary. We play our part in the adventure with ease. And perhaps it is even good for us, for as the characters we are watching are transformed, so, just a little, are we.

—Jean-Claude Carrière

1

2

3

4

5

6

Franco Dragone

A FTER A CHILDHOOD SPENT in the simple beauty of a rural Italian village, Franco left Cairano on December 17, 1958, with his mother Antonietta and his sister Maria. They joined his father Giuseppe, who had been working hard in the coalmines to be able to afford to bring his family over to Belgium.

From then on, Franco played in the streets of La Louvière, Belgium, with bittersweet memories of his childhood in Italy. From Cairano to Las Vegas—the voyage of a lifetime. These few photos show us the beginning of this journey.

♮ **1.** *1963, a family party and a shy smile on his 11th birthday.*

♮ **2.** *1958, newly arrived in Belgium. A mixture of uncertainty and happiness.*

♮ **3.** *The sixties. First suit, first bow tie, first communion.*

♮ **4.** *One day, he believed.*

♮ **5.** *The Great Motorcycle Trial.*

♮ **6.** *Music, friends, and* tutti quanti.

♮ **7.** *Music for and against everything.*

♮ **8.** *On the bridge in La Louvière, music on his mind.*

At home in La Louvière, in this

northern landscape with
its fairytale mists,

Franco dreams up his Las Vegas shows.

La Louvière

AY HAS ALWAYS BEEN a month when odd things happen to me. But being contacted by an Italian who wanted me to go meet him in Belgium, to talk about doing a book on a show in Las Vegas—*that's* never happened before.

We planned to meet in La Louvière, a small mining town pining for its fast-disappearing past.

Our first dinner was at the Auberge de la Louve, where I sat watching this creator of memories. Dragone has been famous for years, all over the world, particularly in Canada and the United States. As I write these lines, three of his shows are playing in Las Vegas. His voice, his entire presence, was unassuming—he almost seemed to apologize for being in the room.

The first thing he said to me was, "I have seen your work. Make this book however you want to." That is typical of Franco: once he has chosen you, he trusts you implicitly. In times when so many decisions are governed by fear, believe me, there is something extraordinary about that. But nothing with him could be ordinary: this was a man on a mad journey, willing to take three hundred people to the other side of the world to make up an entire show. He had a rough outline in his head, but even he didn't know how it was going to end. Up until the last moment, he would change the order of the scenes, reinvent characters, search for costumes. For Franco Dragone, habit makes you lazy. I suppose he thinks it stifles the imagination—so he starts from scratch every day.

But once he has put his trust in you, he expects you to surprise him in return. He is courteous above all other things. He makes sure all those who participate, even in the most minor way, feel that they have the freedom to be inventive. As he said to his company—and this was the first time I had ever heard this from a director—"I will give you some key ideas, but no orders. It's up to you to create your own character. Oh, and if I ask you to do a move which you think is dangerous, don't do it. I'll understand."

On the basis of that dinner together, my decision was made. For the first time in my life, I was looking forward to being part of a company.

§ **Below**
The artists arrive from every continent, and already seem to know each other. It feels like a family reunion, but I am not a member of the family. Not yet.

§ **Facing page**
Franco Dragone in La Louvière.

‡ **Above**
*Franco Dragone
and his artistic
director, Jean Pochoy,
welcome the
company.*

‡ **Right**
*The exhibition hall
in Mons where
rehearsals were held.*

Franco:

"You are not working for me,
I'm working with you!"

Jean Pochoy (in his rather outlandish version of English):

"I listen to you, I am ready to
help with your problem, but I am
not your maman! Forget your ego,
here there are no stars!"

This is what I saw when I arrived

in the morning. Funny, I thought.

Perhaps it's their
way of saying
hello.

Was I expected to do the same?

Estella Undurraga teaches **Zapateo**, the quintessential Argentinean dance. She begins her class with anatomy revision, using a skeleton.

♯ **Preceding double page**
An early morning start: improvisation.
Coach Giuliano Peparini asks them to feel the music, to search for feelings in the deepest part of themselves. I feel a little like a voyeur, watching them. It's nice that they already trust me enough to let me stay in the room.

This hangar was designed for trade fairs and other mercantile endeavors. I think I can say, without risk of contradiction, that the building's developers never imagined it would be filled with this diversity of people from across the globe, all working so hard to purely poetic ends.

Over the coming year,

they will rarely see the light of day.

☿ **Right**
*A pool identical
to the one built
in the theater
in Las Vegas.*

For six months, this structure would be used to rehearse one
of the most dangerous numbers. A few days before the opening
in Las Vegas, Franco was forced to pull it from the show
for the safety of the performers. A big disappointment
for the artists, but the show must go on.

♁ Facing page
*The Tree is a complex
number. Materials
had to be found that
would allow the artists
to hang on to the
wet branches without
slipping.*

♁ Right
*The girls remain
upside down,
heads underwater,
for minutes on end.
Unseen frogmen give
them air.*

The Devil is omnipresent in Franco's show. Is it a throwback to his catholic upbringing, and the stories he must have heard in church as a child in Cairano?

Everywhere you look,

something amazing

is going on. I feel
like I've
landed in a
cross between
an Ivy-league
and a madhouse.

Franco's venture is a condensed version of the United Nations. From the Ukraine to China, from Europe to the

United States, every country is represented.

Lorna: the spirit of the company personified. She has a mature beauty, a fierce determination

I don't know who has her heart, but I hope he knows what he's doing.

toward her work, and courage you just have to admire.

☙ Above and facing page

I was a little apprehensive about asking her to do this.
The floor was concrete; I thought it might not be such a good idea. But she did it without batting an eyelid.
Turn the book around and look at her face—it says more than any explanation of mine.

Steve Wynn

A MERICA, FROM THE POINT OF VIEW OF EVERYWHERE ELSE ON THE PLANET, has long been the land of dreams. But Americans need their dreams too. Here, everything is possible. Steve Wynn, one of the great legends of Las Vegas, is living proof of that.

He understood more than anyone that Vegas was turning into a dead-end town. Gambling—games of chance in name only—would be the death of it. Yet within a few years, thanks to his drive and imagination, it became a playground for Americans of all ages.

First, he built the Mirage, considered by some at the time to be "the greatest success in the history of the world." The next development from this crazy visionary was Treasure Island and then the Bellagio, marking the renewal of a city built on sand, in the middle of the desert, half a century before.

But for this player, that was not enough; with the whole town as his roulette table, he needed one more challenge. With a budget of $2.7 billion dollars, Wynn Las Vegas is the area's biggest construction project ever. That's the sort of fact that makes Steve Wynn want to get up in the morning. Judge for yourself: two thousand seven hundred rooms, a casino covering 110,000 square feet, eighteen restaurants, a 2,087-seat theater, luxury boutiques from all over the world, a golf course, and an art gallery. On the giant screen which has pride of place in front of the hotel, Van Gogh, Monet, Renoir, and Picasso are credited, as if they were actors in Steve Wynn's great film. But if anybody asks him, he answers, "Yes, I bought them, but these works of art don't belong to me, they belong to everybody. I am just their guardian."

For him, the concept of "larger than life" is to be taken literally: "My goal is not to make this complex the best hotel in Las Vegas. My goal is to make it the best hotel on the *planet*."

Seen from the sky, Wynn Las Vegas forms an arc. The next complex he builds, the "Encore," will form the same shape, but the other way around. Astronauts will be able to look down from their satellites and see the two curves forming a letter "S" for Steve. Clearly, this is no ordinary guy. But when you work with stars, you have to aim high.

Simply stated, Steve Wynn is not your average next-door neighbor.

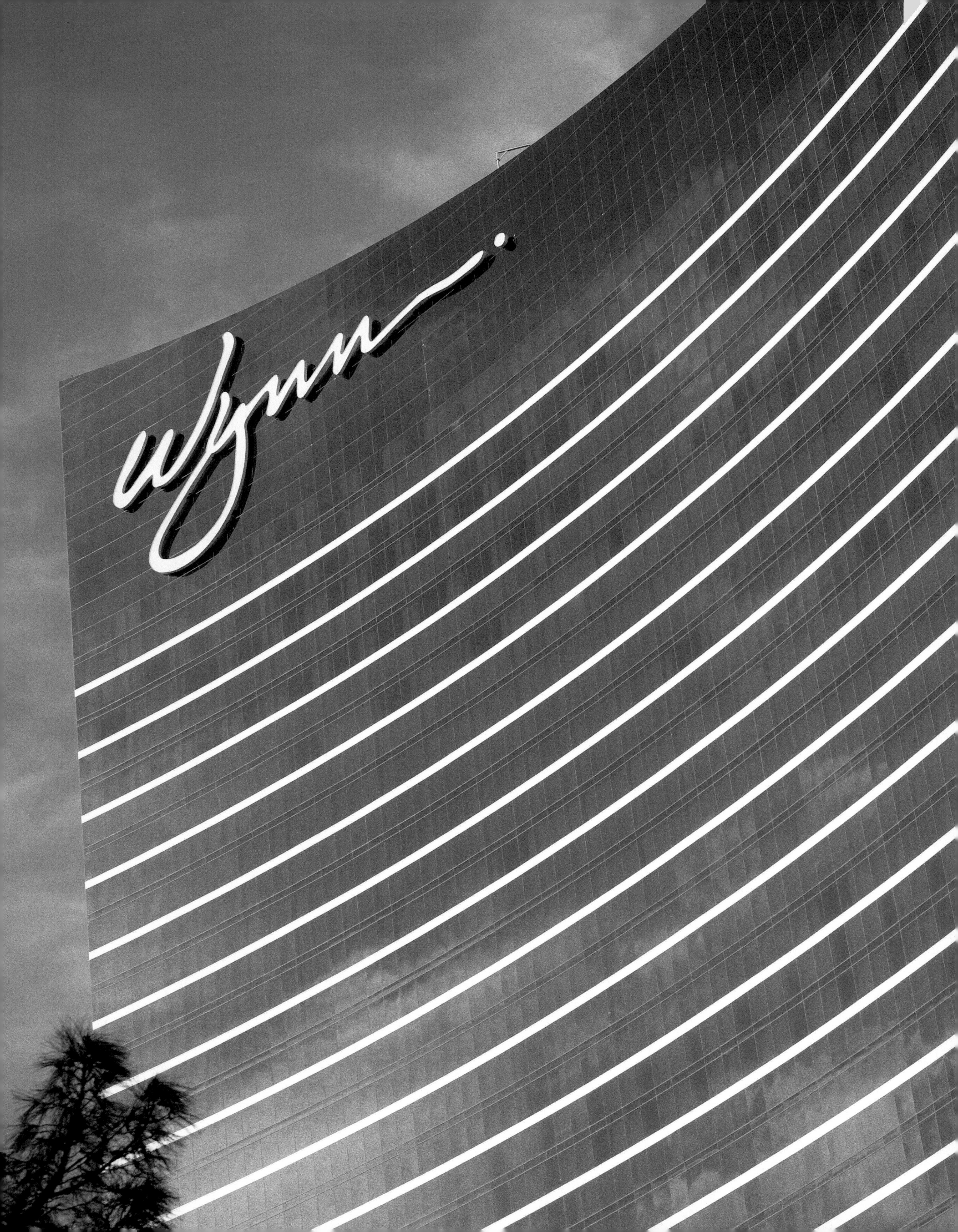
Wynn

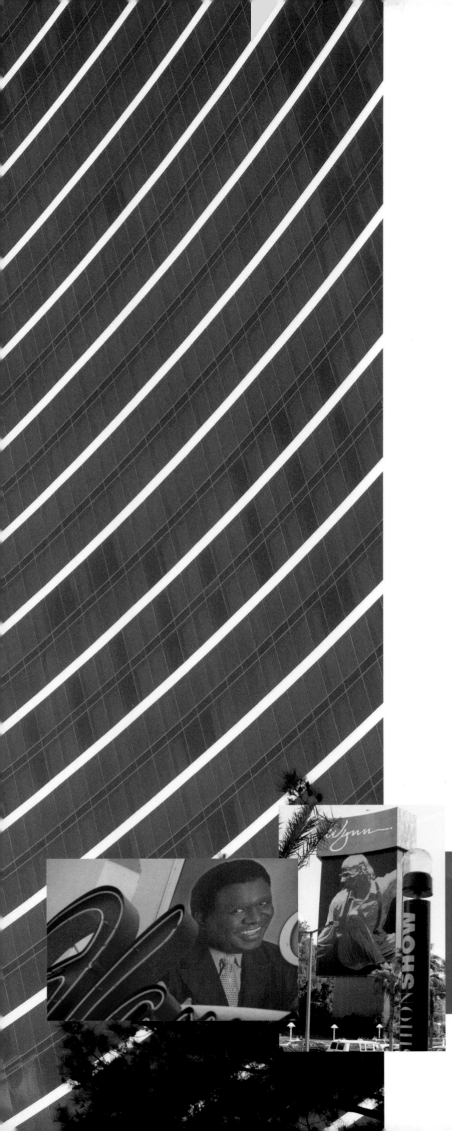

Las Vegas

I FIRST CAME TO LAS VEGAS IN THE
sixties, when it was just one light-
studded street, with carpets on the
sidewalks to draw the customers into the casino
dens. That was when Frank Sinatra and his Rat
Pack ruled the town, and only the young Elvis
Presley came to shake them up. Since the
1980s, and largely due to Steve Wynn, families
from every state have traveled here, eradicating
the atmosphere of a depraved "Sin City" with
the reassuring, "good clean fun" image of an
amusement park for respectable grown-ups.

The majority of Americans never apply for
a passport, but who needs to go abroad when
all you have to do to experience Venice, Cairo,
or Paris is come to Las Vegas?

Shows have always been a major aspect of the Vegas experience. Opposite the Frontier, one of the oldest hotels, the Wynn Las Vegas complex now holds a circular theater built for Franco Dragone's show. Claude Santerre, the site designer, has placed 2,087 seats around a pool measuring almost seventy feet across.

The domed roof of this aquatic theater is eighty feet high.

The pool holds 1.1 million gallons and is twenty-seven feet deep. It takes twelve hours to fill and six to empty. The 86°F water is filtered four times a day.

To have a theater custom-built for just one show is extremely rare. Feasible only in Las Vegas, where the impossible is possible. But it is also perhaps the most straightforward place in the United States because money talks there in such a conspicuous way. There's no uneasiness about it: you only go there to lose it or to win it. If you took the word "dollar" out of the dictionary, Las Vegas would turn back into desert in ten minutes. And everything would disappear, even the dreams.

FIRE SPRINKLER
RISER ROOM

1

2

3

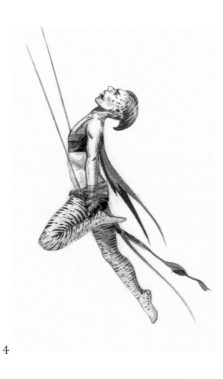

4

6

5

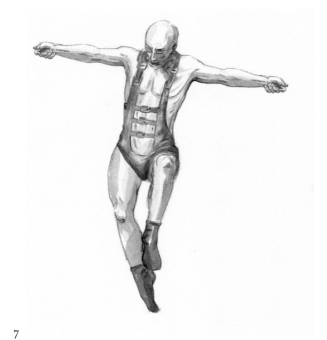

7

8

9

10

11

12

13

14

15

16

17

For this show alone, Claude Renard designed 1,250 costumes and Carmen Arbues Miro designed the make-up.
1. *Bélier écorché (Fleeced ram)*, 2. *Cheval écorché (Flayed horse)*, 3. *Iguane vert (Green iguana)*, 4. *Ailes rouges (Red wings)*, 5. *Champignon (Mushroom)*, 6. *Red Man*, 7. *Show Man*, 8. *Spell*, 9. *Spencer*, 10. *Plante (Plant)*, 11. *Enfant dieu (God-child)*, 12. *Lézard volant (Flying lizard)*, 13. *Didier*, 14. *Dagon*, 15. *Amazone grise (Gray amazon)*, 16. *Apsara*, 17. *Caribou*.

‡ **Above and facing page** Femmes lézards (Lizard Women).

♀ **Facing page**
Enfant dieu
(God-child).

♀ **Right**
Red man.

☙ **Facing page
and right**
Apsaras.

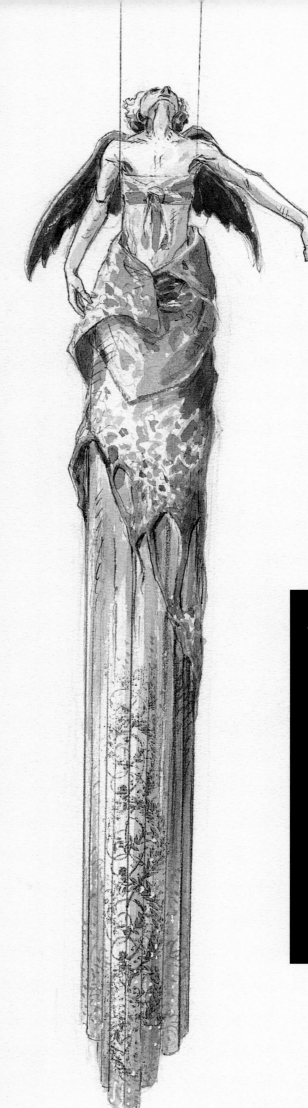

Let
the show
begin.

☧ **Left, above,
and facing page**
Gabriel.

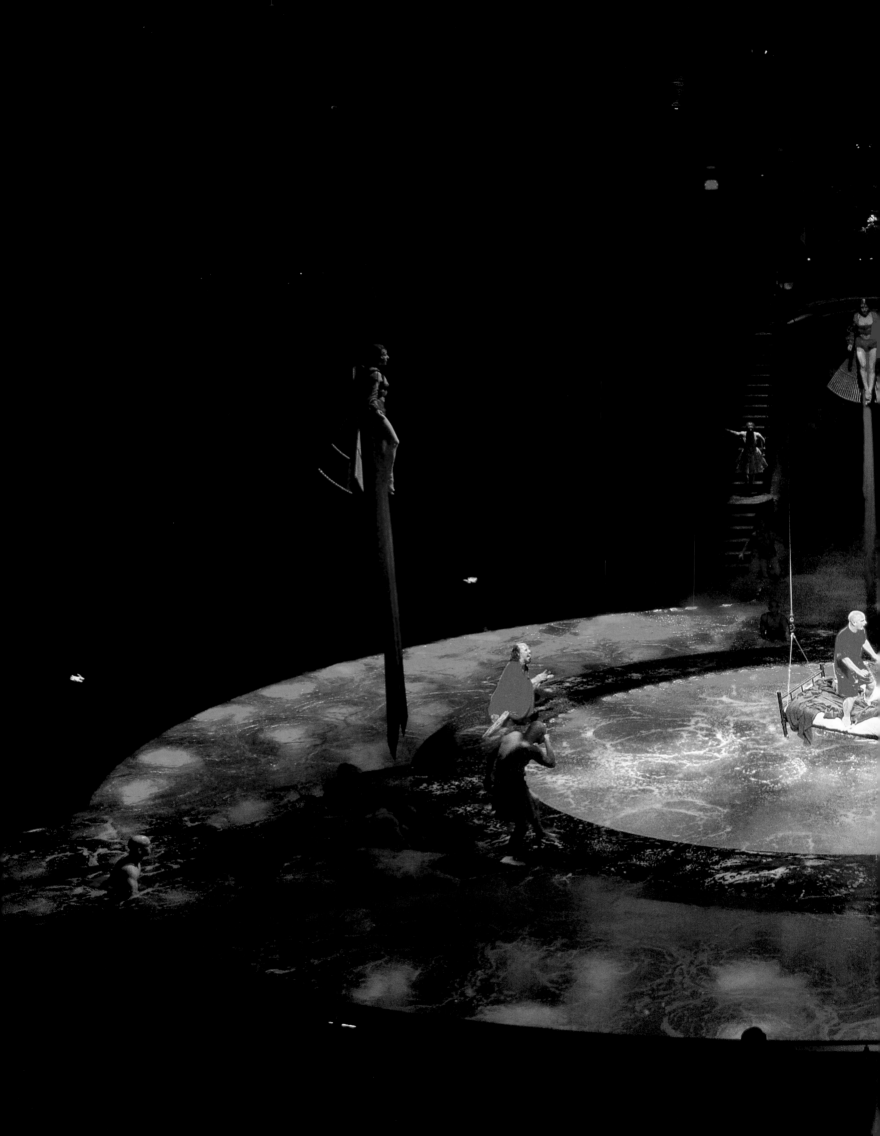

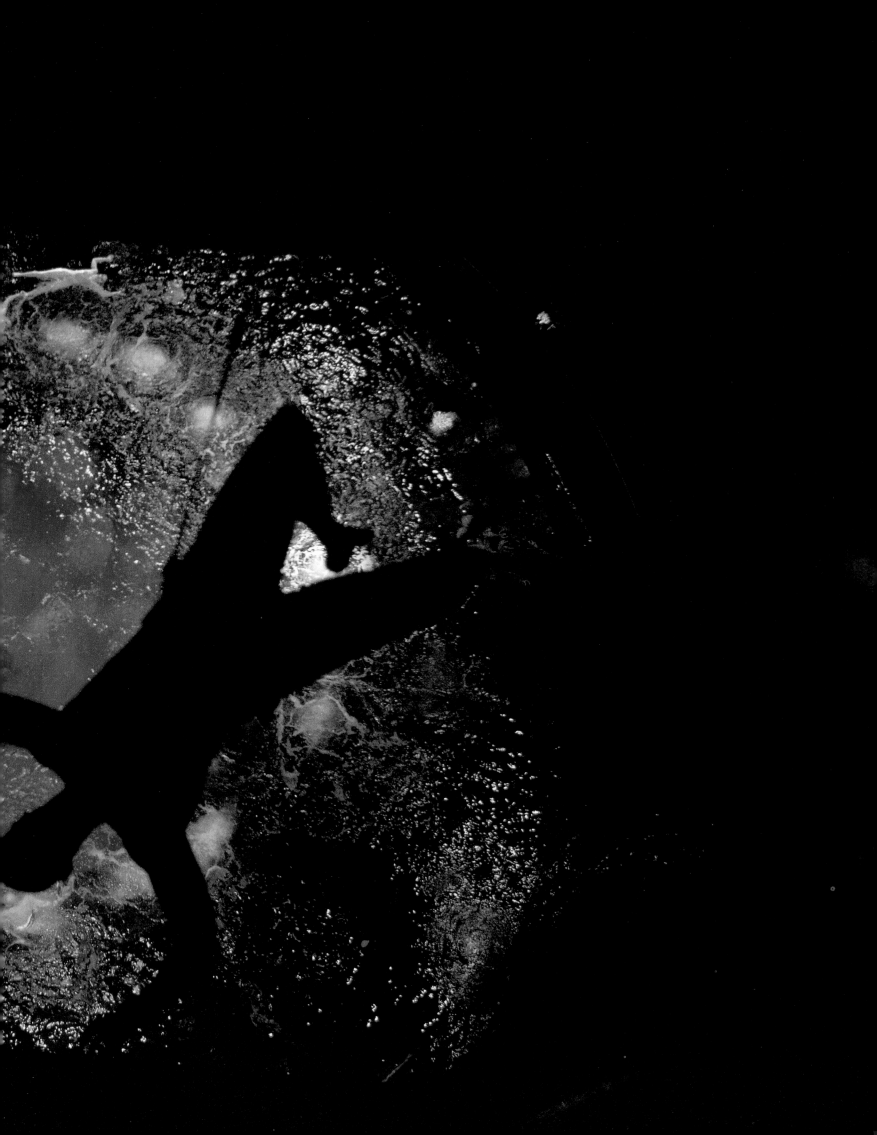

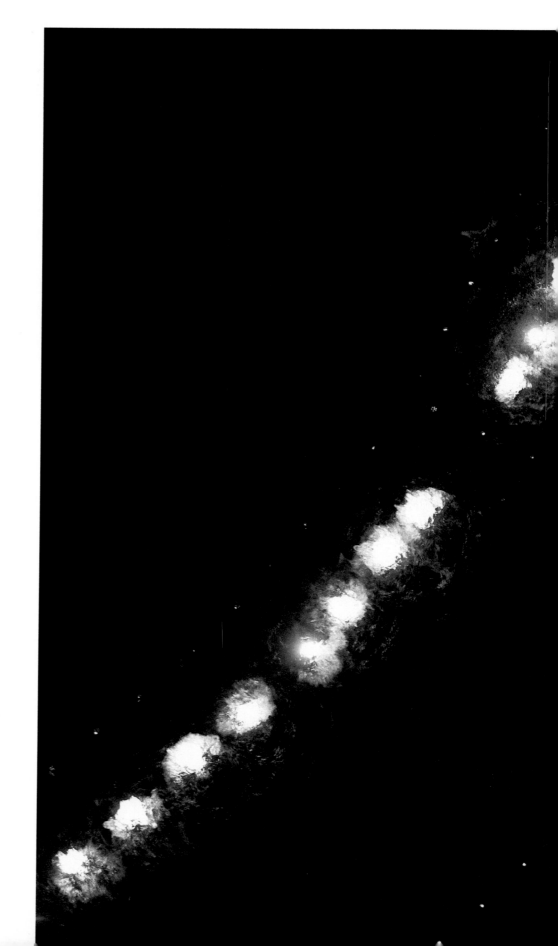

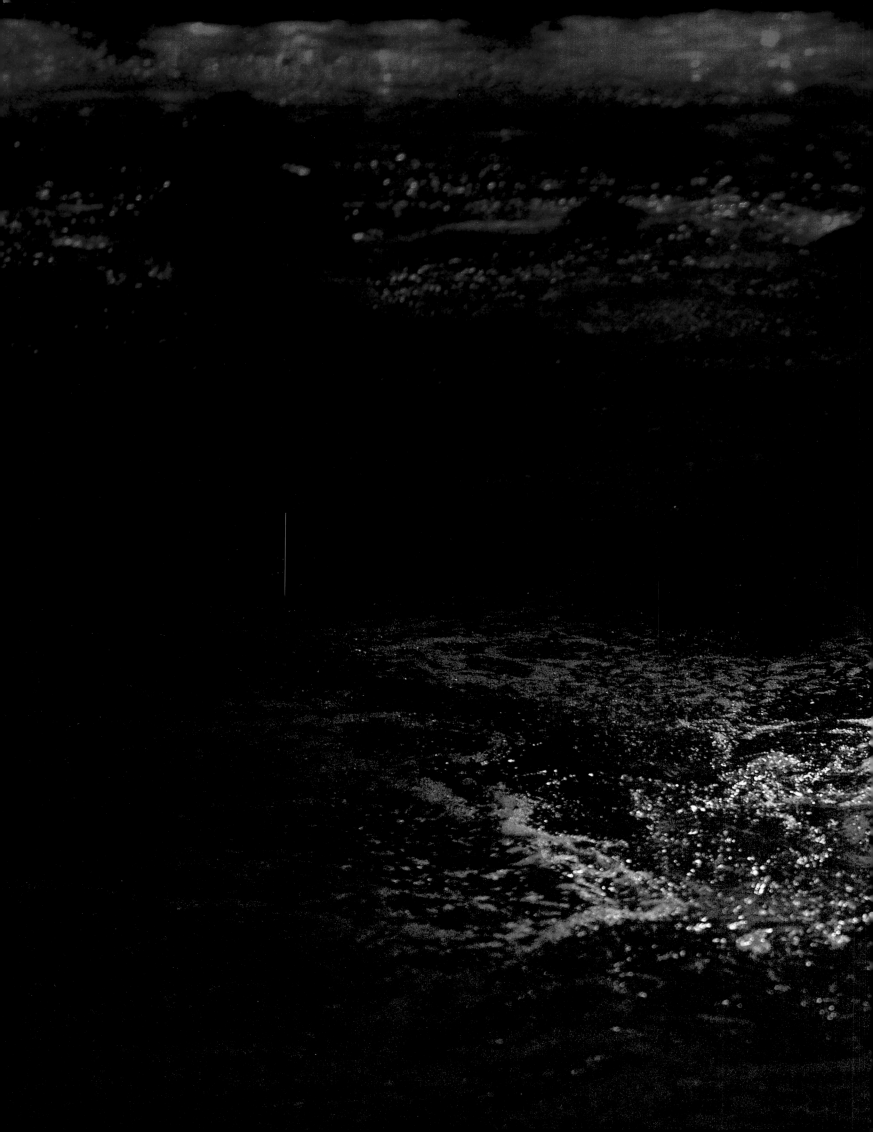

Gallery

FROM WHEN I FIRST SAW THE COSTUMES DESIGNED BY Claude Renard, I wanted to borrow them from Franco's *Le Rêve* and take them on a tour of real life. Into the world of people, or even into my own dreams. I will never be able to sufficiently thank the designers, Carmen Arbues Miro, Janet Grant, and Mark De Coste, for everything they did to make these photographs possible. Pulling artists out of rehearsals, with their hair and make-up done and in costumes specifically designed for a stage environment— and all at the last minute, merely days from opening night when stage fright was at its peak—was no mean feat.

Without the help of Jean Pochoy, Giuliano Peparini, Phyllis Schray, and Michele Trimble, Sophie Aubry and I would not have been able to pull it off.

And finally, Franco. I thank him for having trusted me to take the characters he invented out into the world, without even asking what I was going to do with them.

In the world of show business, where ego so often comes first, that is proof of a rare generosity.

D REAMS OFTEN inspire other dreams. Likewise, when a work is as good as this, it becomes contagious. Characters escape from it, only to pop up elsewhere, provoking further encounters and other collisions of worlds. Confrontations occur that we had not foreseen. Barriers disappear and new perspectives arise.

Jean-Marie Périer followed these escapades with patience and creativity. You'd almost think he had organized them himself.

These are single drops of water splashing out of a great pool. Yet each water droplet embodies the whole dream.

—JEAN-CLAUDE CARRIÈRE

⚲ **Preceding double page**
CHAMPIGNON (MUSHROOM).
The land I call my own.

⚲ **Left**
RED MAN.
Which of these machines is more beautiful?

153

❧ **Right**
LE PALAIS
DE LA BIÈRE
(THE BEER
PALACE).
*A ghostly apparition
from a show they will
never see.*

❧ **Following
double page**
NO ENTRY.
*"I give them nights
to comfort their days."
—Alfred de Vigny.*

⚡ **Above** Elvis. *"Die another day"* meets *"the future waits for no one."*

⚹ **Preceding**
double page
THE VALENTINOS.
Elegance is the art of
appearing to be what you are.

⚹ **Right**
DOWNTOWN.
A look that is full
of the empty town.

162

☙ **Facing page**
RACINE (ROOT).

☙ **Above**
TRUCK.
May the force be with you.

↕ **Right**
PROMISES.
Hope doesn't always keep them.

↕ **Following double page**
THE CAKE.
Remembering Donna Reed.

☙ **Above** BEAST. *When evening falls, under the still-warm sands, a second life begins.*

◊ **Preceding double page**
FRAGILE.
They could lift her to the skies with their pinkies, and she could bring them to their knees with a single look.

◊ **Right**
ROCKING DIDIER.

‡ **Above** GUILTY. *Beauty, the Beast, and the Judeo-Christian.*

↕ **Left**
OLD MAN.
He just keeps rolling along.

↕ **Following
double page**
GABRIEL.
*The meeting of two dreams
against an unchanging sky.*

185

Acknowledgments

SPECIAL THANKS TO:

Pierre Sarazin

Sylvie Flaure / At Large
Agent for
Jean-Marie Périer
www.jean-marie-perier.net

Sophie Aubry
Photographic
Art Direction and
Coordination

Henri Latzarus
Book Design

At Large
Photo Production

**JEAN-MARIE PÉRIER
AND AT LARGE
EXTEND SPECIAL
THANKS TO:**

PARIS

Benoît Grellet
Assistant to
Jean-Marie Périer

Frédéric Lefort
Studio Zéro

BELGIUM

**Philippe Neus,
Catherine Lambert**
La Maison du Tourisme
de La Louvière

Alain Dewier
Musée de la Mine de
Bois-du-Luc

Le Palais de la Bière

TEC transportation

LAS VEGAS

**Jacob Berger,
John Jackson,
Eric Boisteau,
Warren Prewitt, III**
API Productions

Kim Houser-Amaral
Production Services

Ramiro A. Gomez
Producer

Frankie Mason
Wild Streak Talent

Luke Leonard
Photo Assistant

**Bill Fanning
and all the crew**
JR Lighting, Inc.

Wynn Resorts

The New Frontier Hotel

**Valentino and
Beverly Parker**
Valentino's Zootsuit
Connection

Jeff
Count's Kustoms
Specialty Bikes

Vera Petrychenka
Dancer / Singer

**Eldorado Canyon Mine
Tours, Inc.**

The Gladiators
Football Team,
Las Vegas, Nevada

Viva Las Vegas
Themed weddings and
rooms

**Select Trucks of
Las Vegas**

Rony
Accordion Expert

DRAGONE

EXECUTIVE
COMMITTEE

Franco Dragone
Founder and
Artistic Director

Louis Parenteau
President

Patrice Bilodeau
Vice President, Production

Philippe Degeneffe
Vice President,
Corporate Affairs and
Operations

Peter Wagg
Vice President,
Commercial

CREATIVE TEAM

Didier Antoine
Aerial Conceptor

Carmen Arbues Miro
Makeup Designer

Jacky Beffroi
Underwater Designer

Michel Crête
Production Designer

Dirk Decloedt
Assistant Director and
Video Content Designer

John Gilkey
Clown Conceptor

Benoît Jutras
Composer and
Music Director

Daniel Léon
Sound Designer

Dacha Nedorezova
Aquatic Choreographer

Giuliano Peparini
Choreographer

Jean Pochoy
Associate Artistic Director

Claude Renard
Costume Designer

Claude Santerre
Theater Designer and
Stage Designer of the
"Pièce Montée"

Koert Vermeulen
Lighting Designer

CREATIVE
COLLABORATORS

Criss Angel
Creative Collaborator on
Bird and Fire Effects

Yves "Lapin" Aucoin
Collaborator on
Lighting Development

Philippe Chartrand
Collaborator on
Flying Act Development

Mark Goodwin
Lyricist

Ryszard Kruczynski
Gymnastic and
Acrobatic Coach /
Acrobatic Development
Collaborator

Ben Potvin
Collaborator on
Flying Act Development

ARTISTIC TEAM

Leslie Barr
Artistic Coordinator

Phil De Block
Aerial Coach

Janet Grant
Director of Costume
Creation

Paula Holmwood
Assistant Aquatic
Choreographer

Claude Lemay
Director of Casting

Jean Marcouiller
Assistant Production
Designer

Maria "Tony" Pozzobon
Assistant Choreographer

Tomasz Rossa
Assistant Artistic
Coordinator /
High Dive Coach

Virginie Rouyère
Assistant to
Franco Dragone

Phyllis Schray
Production Stage Manager

Anne Tournié
Assistant Choreographer

Yvon Van Lancker
Technical Coordinator

PRODUCTION
DEPARTMENT

Fabrice Bollen
Vice President
Production Associate

Janine Boileau
Accounting Director

Phil Jordan
Coordinator Las Vegas

Jan Mylle
Project Manager

PRODUCTION
COORDINATION

Nathalie Arnoult
Assistant Logistics
Coordinator

**Pierre-Philippe Baeken,
Pierre Lambotte**
Personal Assistants to
Franco Dragone

Koryne Barrette
Assistant to the Vice
President, Commercial

Inneke Didden
Logistics Coordinator

Daniela Fronteddu
Assistant to the Vice
President, Production

Larissa Greuel
Wig Maker and Assistant
to the Makeup Designer

France Hubert
Production and Logistics
Coordinator

Angela Palazzolo
Videographer

Simon Pieret
CDD Managing Director /
Executive Assistant
to Franco Dragone

Shanti Van den Doren
Executive Assistant
to the President

COSTUME TEAM

Mark De Coste
Assistant to Costume
Designer

Joseph Taibi
Manager of Costume
Workshop

Jan Scherry
Head of Wardrobe

Sharon Todaro
Assistant Head of
Wardrobe

WYNN LAS VEGAS

Steve Wynn
Chairman and CEO,
Wynn Resorts

Marc Schorr
President and CEO
Wynn Las Vegas

Rick Gray
General Manager,
Entertainment
Operations

Melanie Kenn
Director of
Cast Relations

Lisa Rayko
Cast Relations Counselor

Imad Kawar
Senior Production
Accountant

Tracy McCollom
Production Accountant

Karen Holm
Receptionist

Dale Hurt
Director of
Technical Operations

Jack Kenn
Assistant Director of
Technical Operations

Karin Swanson
Secretary

Brandon Cox
Public Relations Manager

STAGE MANAGEMENT

Michele Trimble
General Stage Manager

Tracy Lightel
Senior Stage Manager

Damien Long
Stage Manager

Matthew Koenig
Junior Assistant Stage
Manager

PERFORMERS

Jean Ainsley
Drummer, Canada

Didier Antoine
Character, France

Adélaïde Arnaud
Generalist, France

Yann Arnaud
Generalist, France

Rudolf Arnold
Swing, Switzerland

Kerry Atkins
Swimmer, Canada

Benoît Beaufils
Swing, France

Jon Bookout
Generalist, USA

John Brady
Generalist, UK

Tara Brawley
Swimmer, Canada

Claudio Carneiro
Clown, Brazil

Maurizia Cecconi
Swimmer, Italy

Pauline Chydzinski
Generalist, France

Dane Clarke
Generalist, UK

Gregg Curtis
Generalist, USA

Jean-François Cyr
Guitarist, Canada

Michel Cyr
Band Leader
Musical Director, Canada

Alberto Del Campo
Generalist, Spain

Rob Falsini
Singer, Italy

Geneviève Garneau
Generalist, Canada

Victor Gathing
Generalist, USA

Mirela Golinska
Generalist, Poland

Paul Herzfeld
Generalist, France

Paula Holmwood
Swimmer, Canada

Suzanna Hyatt
Swimmer, USA

Véronique Jean
Generalist, Canada

Hérelle Jegoux
Swimmer, France

Dariusz Jochymek
Swing, Poland

Sean Kempton
Clown, UK

Tatiana Klepatsky
Generalist, Ukraine

Natalie Kourpa
Generalist, UK

Veronica Lachance
Swimmer, Canada

Marcin Lominski
Generalist, Poland

Amélie Lupien
Character, Canada

Ryan Lyons
Generalist, Canada

Richie Maguire
Generalist, USA

Amélie Major
Generalist, Canada

Sergiy "Fox" Malyarov
Generalist, Ukraine

Allan McCormick
Generalist, Canada

Alison Mixon
Character, USA

Sarah Molasky
Generalist, USA

Andrey Moraru
Character, Ukraine

Gonzalo Muñoz Ferrer
Clown, Colombia

Frédérick Nicolas
Generalist, France

Mirek Niepielski
Generalist, Poland

Michaela O'Connor
Swing, Australia

Daniel Passer
Clown, USA

Paul Pelletier
Keyboard, Canada

Ludivine Perrin
Swimmer, France

Christopher Phi
Swing, USA

Ben Potvin
Generalist, Canada

Tomasz Prokop
Generalist, Poland

Monica Riba
Generalist, Spain

Grzegorz Ros
Generalist, Poland

Jessica Ros
Swimmer, France

Julia Sardella
Swimmer, France

Leah Schachar
Swimmer, Canada

Kelly Shaylor
Generalist, UK

Paul Shihadeh
Bassist, Canada

Jim Slonina
Clown, USA

Lorna Somner
Generalist, UK

Adrian Stan
Generalist, Romania

Kate St. Pierre
Singer, USA

Raman Stsepaniuk
Generalist, Belarus

Carmen Tausend
Generalist, USA

Marie Tavenard
Swimmer, France

Kent Thomson
Generalist, Canada

David Underwood
Generalist, UK

Daniela Vairo
Generalist, Italy

Thao Vilayvong
Generalist, France

Sam Welbourn
Generalist, UK

Tomasz "Wilu" Wilkosz
Generalist, Poland

Wayne Wilson
Clown, USA

Sebastian Zarkowski
Generalist, Poland

Andrzej Zumanow
Generalist, Poland

GALLERY PERFORMERS

Dane Clarke
Champignon (Mushroom)
Red Man

Amélie Lupien
Le Palais de la Bière

Natalie Kourpa
No Entry

Geneviève Garneau
Elvis

Gregg Curtis
The Valentinos

Sarah Molasky
Downtown

Monica Riba
Racine (Root)

Mirek Niepielski
Truck

**Wayne Wilson,
Jim Slonina,
Sean Kempton,
Daniel Passer,
Claudio Carneiro**
Madame Rêve

**Monica Riba,
Sergiy "Fox" Malyarov**
The Pool

Julia Sardella
Promises

Gonzalo Muñoz Ferrer
The Cake

Sophie Aubry
Beast

Tatiana Klepatsky
Fragile

Didier Antoine
Rocking Didier

Allan McCormick
Guilty

**Sergiy "Fox" Malyarov,
Dariusz Jochymek**
Planet

Andrey Moraru
Old Man

Michaela O'Connor
Gabriel

Translated from the French by Joseph West
Typesetting: Barbara Kekus
Proofreading: Helen Adedotun
Color separation: 4 Coul'

Distributed in North America by Rizzoli International Publications, Inc.

Published simultaneously in French as *Le Rêve*
© Éditions Flammarion, 2005
English-language edition
© Éditions Flammarion, 2005

05 06 07 4 2 3 I

FC0503-05-IX
ISBN: 2-0803-0503-4
Dépôt légal: 09/2005

Printed in Barcelona, Spain, by Egedsa.